The Litterbug

Contents

1

Chapter 1 Wonderland

The workmen had packed away their tools and gone. Everything was finished. The old house and its gardens which had stood on this spot for so many years had now been turned into an Animal Park. Everything was neat and clean. There was the smell of freshly-cut grass and wet paint.

Tom and Kate were going exploring, and the first place they intended to visit was the big glass and metal dome, which was sparkling in the sunlight. The main doors were wide open. The two children slipped inside.

What they saw on the other side of the doors made them gasp in astonishment. They had entered a Wonderland! Stretching out before them was a glittering, shimmering blue pool. At one end of the pool, little waves lapped on a yellow sandy beach, and the children could see that the pool got deeper and deeper as it went farther out.

In the middle of the pool a jumble of rocks stuck up from the water. The rocks were hard and solid, but the children could see gaps and cracks where small plants and trees had been planted. At one side of the rocks a gurgling waterfall tumbled down.

All around the pool were tropical plants and small trees. They were planted in rich brown flower beds, wooden barrels, terracotta pots and hanging baskets. There was every shade of green you could wish to see, and brilliantly coloured flowers of scarlet, blue and orange.

Brightly-coloured insects flitted in and out of the flowers. Professor Quickly had not collected any insects in Brazil, but thousands of insect eggs had been stuck to the leaves and bark of the plants he had collected, and now they had all hatched out.

The two children wandered into the plants and trees. It was just like being in the Brazilian jungle, though it was not so dark. Their nostrils were filled with wonderful smells from the flowers, and every now and then they had to duck as the beating wings of an insect brushed past them.

It took quite a long time to go right round the dome, because they kept stopping to look at the plants and insects.

In the end they arrived back at the little sandy beach. They sat down for a rest, and dipped their feet in the water.

'It's just wonderful,' said Kate. 'What a pity the gleeks aren't here to see it all.'

'But we are!' squeaked a gleek. 'Where have you two been?'

Tom and Kate nearly jumped out of their skins as the entire family of gleeks suddenly surrounded them. They were still alive!

'However did you get away from the bulldozer?' gasped Kate.

'We had to move very fast,' they said. 'The tunnel caved in, and we hid in the woods until we could find somewhere else to live.'

'But where are you living now?' asked Tom. The gleeks nodded toward the big heap of rocks in the middle of the pond. 'Our den is in the middle of those rocks. But the pond is too deep for us to tunnel underneath it, so we have to swim to the bank every time we come out. We get very wet!'

Tom's eyes twinkled. 'I think we might be able to help you with that,' he said. 'Come on Kate!' and the two children dashed off to their house.

The Professor was still chatting to Adam and Polly when they got back.

'Did you like the tropical house?' asked the Professor.

'Brilliant!' said Tom.

'Fantastic!' said Kate, 'but we can't stay, we're going back there in a minute!'

The two children dashed up to their bedrooms. Seconds later they were flying out of the door again, and heading back to the pool.

'Well, that seems to have made them happy at last.' smiled the Professor.

'Thank goodness!' said Polly and Adam.

Two minutes later the gleeks were sailing round the pool in Tom's model boat!

Chapter 2 The animals arrive

For Tom and Kate, the next week passed in a flash. They spent their days wandering around the Animal Park, and played with the gleeks in the evening.

The gleeks worked every day looking after all the living things in the grounds, and keeping everything neat and well-kept.

At night they loved to go back to the tropical house, because it was nearly as good as going home to the rain forests of Brazil. They called it their 'home from home'. They had even built a hidden boat-house for Tom's model boat. Everyone was happy.

Then came the bright sunny morning when all the animals arrived. Once more a line of heavy trucks came chugging up the drive and pulled to a stop outside Crack Puzzle House.

The Professor jumped out of the first truck.

'Come on!' he shouted. 'Let's get them all unloaded!'

The rest of the day was extremely hectic. Everyone was in a rush. The animals had to be unloaded, fed and watered, then taken to different parts of the grounds.

It was very hard work, and many of the animals were confused and upset.

'It will take a long time for them to settle in,' said the Professor. 'We won't let the public in until all our animals feel happy and safe.'

But the Professor did not know about the gleeks. That night, when everyone was in bed, the gleeks crept out of the tropical house and visited every animal in the grounds. They stroked them, and whispered to them, and even the most timid animal soon settled down.

And the next day, everyone was amazed to see that all the animals were contented and settled. It was if they had been living there for years!

Chapter 3 Grand Opening Day

Everything went so well that it was just
two weeks later that the day of the
Grand Opening arrived. The Professor had
taken on extra staff to help out, and they
all looked very smart in their green outfits.

The sun was shining in a blue sky and
hundreds of visitors were coming through the
freshly-painted gates.

It did not take long to work out that the Animal Park was going to be a big hit. The visitors loved it. They had been used to visiting zoos where all the animals were kept locked up.

But this place was different. These animals were so tame and trusting that the visitors could get close enough to stroke them. And all the animals looked fit and well, with glossy coats, cold wet noses and bright eyes.

At the end of that first day, when the very last tired and happy visitor had left and everyone else had gone to bed, the gleeks crept out to inspect the grounds. The moon was shining brightly, lighting up the lawns and trees, and the gleeks were able to see quite well.

What they saw made them sad and upset. Many of the visitors had spent the day trampling all over the grounds, dropping litter and flattening plants. The grounds were a complete and utter mess!

Sadly, the gleeks picked everything up.

Chapter 4 More work for the gleeks

As time passed by, more and more visitors came to the Park. Crowds of fussy children tumbled out of cars and coaches, bored stiff from sitting still for so long.

The gleeks were pleased to see happy children, but they knew that where there were children, there was mess.

The gleeks did not complain, they just got on with the job of keeping their gardens neat and clean. Every night, when everyone had gone home, the gleeks slipped out of the tropical house and started to clean up.

At dawn each morning, when everyone was still asleep, the gleeks were just finishing! They worked right through the night, tending the trees and plants, soothing the animals, picking up litter and getting rid of it.

Working on these 'night shifts' was much more difficult than working in the day. The gleeks missed working in the bright sunlight. But they knew it was impossible to work in the day-time. The visitors would be sure to spot them as they moved around.

When all the work was finished, and the sun was just coming up, the tired gleeks trooped back into the dome. This was the best part of the day. There was still nobody about, and they had the entire dome to play in.

The first thing they did was to jump into the cool, fresh water and clean themselves up. Then they spent a little time playing games in the bushes and trees and the pool itself.

Then, before the staff started work the gleeks crept back into their tunnel, shut the hidden door firmly behind them, and fell into a deep, deep sleep.

Only Tom and Kate knew what was going on, and they felt sorry for the gleeks.

'The least we can do is make sure that they get plenty to eat,' said Kate.

'Yes,' agreed Tom. 'They love lots of sweet things, but how are we going to do it?'

'We must trust Dad!' said Kate.
Tom nodded, and they went to see him.

'Well I never!' said Dad when he had heard their story. 'Whoever would have thought it! I knew that there was something funny going on when you built that hide.'

'So will you help us Dad?' asked Tom.

'And never, never, NEVER tell anyone else?' added Kate. Dad thought for a minute.

'Yes, I will,' he said, 'because after all, these little creatures are helping me to do my job, so they should get something in return!'

And every night after that, when the gleeks came back from their night shift, there was a little brown sack at the side of the pool full of good things to eat.

Chapter 5 The Litterbug comes home

The Litterbug was on his way home. He had spent nearly a year travelling around Britain, and he'd left at least twenty towns looking like rubbish tips. But he was feeling tired and he needed a rest.

Before long, he was standing outside the main gates of Crack Puzzle Animal Park. He looked through the metal bars for a long, long time. He saw the neat, green lawns, the well-swept pathways, the sturdy trees, the colourful flowers, and the big glittering dome, full of clean panes of glass.

'Wow!' he whispered to himself. 'What's been happening here? Everything's so neat! I've never seen anything like it.'

He forgot all about being tired. His eyes lit up and his mouth curved in a wicked smile. He wiped his nose on the back of his hand and said to himself,

'This needs thinking about. Here's a job that should be done properly. This job is so good it may be the last one I ever do!'

The Litterbug went to find his cave. Luckily, it was still hidden by plants, bushes and tree branches. No-one knew that the cave was there.

The Litterbug crept inside. It was dark and dirty, and there was a nasty smell, but the Litterbug liked that. Then he saw a family of bats hanging from the roof of the cave. They would have to go. He picked up a stick. The unlucky bats never knew what hit them. There was a loud THWACK, then a rattle of wings as the frightened bats came flying out of the cave.

The Litterbug spent the rest of the day making some doors for the front of the cave out of branches and twigs. He wanted to make sure that the bats could not get back in, and that nobody would be able to see inside the cave once he started to put things in it. And he planned to put lots of things in it!

By the time he had finished, the doorway to the cave was difficult to see.

It was past midnight when the Litterbug crept out of the tunnel, stretched, wiped his nose again and had a good look round.

'Time to eat,' he muttered. Very quietly, he slipped out of the cave and moved towards the glass dome.

Suddenly, the Litterbug stopped. He could see some little creatures scuttling about in the darkness. He hid behind a tree trunk, and looked out.

'This place is full of surprises,' the Litterbug whispered. 'But they'll all get a BIG surprise before I've finished!'

Very quietly, without disturbing the gleeks, the Litterbug went on towards the dome. He was starving, and he needed to find some food fast. Soon he was inside the dome, looking in amazement at the shimmering blue pool and the lush, green trees.

'Wow!' he said again.

He'd never seen anything like it.

'This job is going to be bigger than ever. I'm going to have terrific fun in here.'

Now he looked for something to eat. One of the trees had some funny-looking cones on it. The Litterbug tried one. It was sour.

'Yuk!' he yelled, spitting it out into the pool. 'That's no good.' He went on with his hunt and at last he found a small brown sack standing on the sand. He opened it up and looked inside. His eyes lit up.

Ten minutes later he was on his way back to his cave, feeling happy and content.

Chapter 6 The gleeks get a shock

At sunrise, the gleeks marched back to the dome. They were tired after working on the night shift, and they were looking forward to a splash in the pool and a bite to eat.

Chatting happily, they went into the dome. But as soon as they saw the pool they stopped in horror. It was a complete and utter mess. Floating on top of the water were bits of orange and apple peel, empty tins and jars, soggy packets and the empty brown sack. All around the pool were muddy footprints and there were filthy handprints all over the panes of glass on the lower part of the dome. Scrawled in mud on the yellow sand were the words,

'Surprise, surprise!'

The gleeks were shocked and upset. Some of the little ones began to cry.

The gleeks knew that they couldn't just leave the place in that state. Even though they were tired and hungry, they set about cleaning everything up before the first visitors arrived.

They pulled out the little boat from the boat house, and used nets and sticks to collect all the rubbish which was floating about on the pool.

They went into the tool room in their den and came out with mops, scrubbing brushes, little wooden ladders, buckets and cloths. Then they set to work, mopping up the muddy footprints and cleaning and polishing the panes of glass on the dome.

It was very hard work, but they did it just before the first members of staff arrived to begin their day's work. Then the tired and unhappy gleeks crept down into their tunnel. They had to go to bed without anything to eat.

Chapter 7 The picnic

The Litterbug was getting everything ready.
Messing up the Animal Park was going to be
his last job and he wanted it to be perfect.
He knew that he had to plan it properly, and
that he had to get together all the things he
needed. He spent a lot of time travelling far
and wide, collecting anything which he thought
would be useful.

He visited gardens, backyards, empty
houses, building sites, rubbish tips, canal
banks and even a factory on an industrial
estate, to gather the things he needed.

It would take a while to get everything ready, so the Litterbug planned to spend some time upsetting the visitors to the Park. He prowled around the grounds, flitting from tree to tree and from rock to rock, looking for mischief. And it did not take long to find his victims!

Looking out from behind a tree trunk one sunny afternoon, he spotted a family who had just settled down to have a picnic. Mum and Dad had set everything out, and the children were sitting politely waiting to begin. Everyone had been looking forward to this picnic for a long time. Soon they were all tucking in, and they were amazed to see some little birds that were tame enough to come and eat with them.

Then just as Mum and Dad were struggling to open the bottle of wine, the Litterbug struck. There was a quick blur, and then everything seemed to happen at once!

What a shame! One minute everyone was happy, and the next minute birds were squawking, the jelly exploded, drinks fell to the ground, cakes and buns went flying, and Dad got splattered with ketchup!

It was the same all over the park. No-one was safe from the Litterbug, and it wasn't long before the Professor heard all about it.

Chapter 8 The Professor calls a meeting

It was not long before the Professor began to get complaints from the visitors. And he knew just who was responsible for all the mess. The Litterbug had come back!

The Professor called a meeting of all the staff. Tom and Kate went along, and they smuggled one of the gleeks in with them, hidden in a carrier bag.

The Professor told the staff all about the Litterbug, and asked them all to keep their eyes open and to report anything odd.

'We've got to track down this little monster,' he said, 'before everyone stops coming to the Park!'

As soon as the staff left the meeting they started to look for the Litterbug, but he was fast asleep inside his cave where nobody could find him.

The gleek who had hidden in the carrier bag went back to discuss things with the others.

'We must give up working on the gardens for a little while and look for the Litterbug,' he told them. 'We can split up the Park between us, and find places to hide. Then we must watch and wait. One of us is sure to see something.'

'Brilliant!' shouted another gleek.

'And we mustn't forget the other animals who live here. We must ask them to help us too.'

So the gleeks did not do any gardening and cleaning that night. And the next day, all around the Park, little eyes were watching.

The gleeks were sure that it was only a matter of time before they spotted the Litterbug, but they were in for a sad shock. The Litterbug was far too clever and quick to fall into a trap.

As soon as the Litterbug came out into the Park he saw that the gleeks were watching out for him. It did not take him long to spot them hiding in trees, on the roofs of buildings, or behind plants and bushes. The gleeks were extremely clever at hiding, but the Litterbug could still see their glittering eyes.

The Litterbug was angry and cross, and he forgot all about his big plan for a while. The gleeks were asking for it. He would teach them a lesson they would never forget! He moved at the speed of light back to his hidden cave. Very quickly, he collected some things together, then, as quick as a flash, he was off again, grinning happily.

Chapter 9 The sparks fly

The Litterbug started with the gleeks who were hidden in the trees and bushes. They just didn't know what hit them! One by one they came crashing and tumbling to the ground as branches snapped, or well-aimed stones hit them on the head, or an invisible hand gave them a push.

The gleeks on the roof-tops were next. The Litterbug set out a line of milk bottles, opened a box of fireworks and took out some matches. He slid rockets into the necks of the milk bottles, and aimed them at the roof-tops. He lit a match and held it to the twist of blue paper which stuck out from each rocket. Then, while the twists of blue paper were still slowly burning, he grabbed a handful of jumping crackers and set off again. Suddenly, the sky was full of flames and showers of sparks of every colour.

The frightened gleeks closed their eyes and jumped.

Very sadly, the battered and frightened gleeks got up and limped back to the dome. But when they got there, they were in for another shock. The gleeks shuddered. They wondered what the Litterbug planned to do next.